CATS

A BOOK OF 21 POSTCARDS

BROWNTROUT PUBLISHERS
SAN FRANCISCO • CALIFORNIA

BROWNTROUT PUBLISHERS

P.O. BOX 280070
SAN FRANCISCO • CALIFORNIA 94128-0070
800 938 7688

ISBN: 1-56313-770-4
TITLE #: P5770

BROWNTROUT publishes a large line of calendars, photographic books, and postcard books.
Please write for more information.

Printed in Korea

CATS

BROWNTROUT PUBLISHERS, INC.   P.O. BOX 280070   SAN FRANCISCO, CA 94128

CATS

BROWNTROUT PUBLISHERS, INC.   P.O. BOX 28070   SAN FRANCISCO, CA 94128

CATS

BROWNTROUT PUBLISHERS, INC.   P.O. BOX 280070   SAN FRANCISCO, CA 94128

CATS

BROWNTROUT PUBLISHERS, INC. P.O. BOX 280070 SAN FRANCISCO, CA 94128

CATS

BROWNTROUT PUBLISHERS, INC. P.O. BOX 280070 SAN FRANCISCO, CA 94128

CATS

BROWNTROUT PUBLISHERS, INC. P.O. BOX 280070 SAN FRANCISCO, CA 94128

CATS

BROWNTROUT PUBLISHERS, INC.   P.O. BOX 280070   SAN FRANCISCO, CA 94128

CATS

BROWNTROUT PUBLISHERS, INC.   P.O. BOX 280070   SAN FRANCISCO, CA 94128

CATS

BROWNTROUT PUBLISHERS, INC.   P.O. BOX 280070   SAN FRANCISCO, CA 94128

CATS

BROWNTROUT PUBLISHERS, INC.   P.O. BOX 280070   SAN FRANCISCO, CA 94128

CATS

BROWNTROUT PUBLISHERS, INC.   P.O. BOX 280070   SAN FRANCISCO, CA 94128

CATS

BROWNTROUT PUBLISHERS, INC. P.O. BOX 280070 SAN FRANCISCO, CA 94128

CATS

BROWNTROUT PUBLISHERS, INC.   P.O. BOX 280070   SAN FRANCISCO, CA 94128

CATS

BROWNTROUT PUBLISHERS, INC.   P.O. BOX 280070   SAN FRANCISCO, CA 94128

CATS

BROWNTROUT PUBLISHERS, INC.   P.O. BOX 280070   SAN FRANCISCO, CA 94128

CATS

BROWNTROUT PUBLISHERS, INC.   P.O. BOX 280070   SAN FRANCISCO, CA 94128

CATS

BROWNTROUT PUBLISHERS, INC.   P.O. BOX 280070   SAN FRANCISCO, CA 94128

CATS

BROWNTROUT PUBLISHERS, INC.   P.O. BOX 280070   SAN FRANCISCO, CA 94128

CATS

BROWNTROUT PUBLISHERS, INC.　P.O. BOX 280070　SAN FRANCISCO, CA 94128

CATS

BROWNTROUT PUBLISHERS, INC.   P.O. BOX 280070   SAN FRANCISCO, CA 94128

CATS

BROWNTROUT PUBLISHERS, INC. P.O. BOX 280070 SAN FRANCISCO, CA 94128